NOOK SACK

Poems
& Prose

Rick Hermann

Bellingham, Washington

The poem "Nooksack" was first published in *Poetry Walk: Sue C. Boynton Contest, The Second Five Years* (2015). "Rain" appeared in the *11th Annual Sue Boynton Poetry Contest, 2016 Winning Poems* (2016). "Me & Woody Guthrie" was published in *Noisy Waters: Poetry from Whatcom County, Washington* (ed. Luther Allen & J.J. Kleinberg, 2016). "Crossing the Border" was first published in *Borders,* an anthology of stories and poems written by residents of Whatcom County (2011).

Cover painting by Rick Hermann, acrylic on cedar, based on a series of Coast Salish paintings found on a tavern wall in Seattle's Pioneer Square district just prior to the building's demolition in 1974.

Unless otherwise identified, all drawings are by Rick Hermann.

Back cover drawing, "Bird's Nest" by James Acord, 1979. Used with permission.

Prepress services by Kathleen Weisel, Bellingham, WA (weiselcreative.com)

Contents

Part Three: *Telling the Story*

Preface

Nooksack is a River, a People, a Spirit of Place abiding in dark, deep, fern-choked ravines, up wooded slopes and ridges, descending again to lowlands where a few stands of old growth fir and hemlock survive. Nooksack is shadow and cloud as well as bright glacial ice far above the Salish Sea. Nooksack, as an incarnation of Nature, as well as an expression of Spirit in human beings, figures large in the lives of many occupying what was once the province of Coast Salish tribes in what we now call Northwestern Washington.

Nooksack is also a Mother, one who would have her children find the strength and wisdom to survive catastrophe and tragedy, and even then to continue living. Impassive and tireless, she can impart courage, literally working her fingers into our bones to revive us from dreams of despair and find new beginnings.

I hope this feeling, or sense, carries through the book, even though most of the works included here are not directly concerned (although some are) with the qualities and significance of Nooksack as a presence in our contemporary life.

Validation of one's work is invaluable. I acknowledge and appreciate the many individuals who have encouraged my efforts. Especially, for generosity through long friendship and shared love of books and reading, I thank Leslie Tregillus and Tom Jones.

The comments (and sometimes silences) from members of my Parkinson's disease support group, after I read them something new, also inspire me to keep trying. We listen well to one another.

And kudos to the organizers and poets who co-create the annual Sue C. Boynton poetry contest in Whatcom County—what wonderful poems, each its own world. Year after year.

My wife, Lee Willis, a poet of Tai Chi and Qigong, has given of herself on my behalf in too many ways to enumerate here. In addition to being my staunchest ally, toughest critic, and most true friend and loving life partner, she is my compassionate caregiver. "Caregiver, Beloved," the second poem in this volume, is gratefully and lovingly dedicated to her.

Part One

Good Reasons To Stay Alive

"Angels affect us oft, and worshipped be."

~John Donne

Nooksack

On the flood
of the spring melt,
this river mothers me,
works her fingers
into my bones,
rocks me.
Coming cold
off the glacier,
she closes
her flashing eyes at night,
dreamless, cool,
urgent.
There are reasons
to live, she tells me.
Good reasons
to stay alive.

Caregiver, Beloved

Though help is needed yet,
a portion of love's balm
is your caress.

When I need hands,
your hands come alive,
your arms embrace.

Our eyes
know everything
our barren skin has seen.

Such feelings flee the omens
of desire; in life with simple love
no heart will break.

Thus do we invent our world.
With touching hands we do our
love beget, a lasting love

that leaves no mark or trace
when tides turn 'round
and love is turned to grace.

7/20/2014

I am stuck. The weather is staying hot (some would call it merely warm), and I am stuck. Stuck with my observance of my borderline agoraphobia, my fears around climate change, my apathy about writing anything because it's too hard and it's all been said by now—surely there is a sufficiency of words in the world. I'm stuck in thoughts of my sister's death, when I saw her the last time and she was so sick and sickly, about the poem I wrote about her that is so dismissive of any depth to our relationship. Stuck in Parkinson's. Stuck with people who have died and whose memorial services I have attended, actually comparing the large number of people who were present at those events to my estimate of the meager few my passing might attract. I am stuck in the heat of fear—of change, aging, progressing, losing, dying. I try to lay down these fears like a book I don't want to continue, or maybe put it aside until I feel a little more positive about things.

And that can change. It always does. Whenever I am "off" (referring to the minutes or hours between doses when symptom-controlling medications are not working, as happens in later stages of the disease), everything is depressed: movement, will, love, hope, sense of what's possible. Because I know in the darkness of these bad moments that I will not stay here, and that everything is not only possible but attainable and likely to occur.

So I look at all the ways of thinking, responding, reacting, and behaving in my stuckness, and, if I can just get so much as a crack between the wall and the door, I can see inside myself and realize that the way to overcome fear of death is to practice dying as I would practice a meditation. That dying is no more than not taking the next in-breath. I lie still, just breathing, in and out, in and out, realizing that this is not so hard. If I can feel safe in my breathing, I can face the last exhale when the time comes.

Maybe this sounds morbid, or suicidal, but I don't see it that way. I see practicing dying being a tool that I can use to help me to a perfectly safe, bodiless place—whether that is consciousness or not-consciousness. Not as a plan for self-obliteration.

All the things that I can be stuck about comprise my personal narrative as informed by my roles, relationships, thoughts, feelings, desires, fears, and memory. Getting unstuck is a process of easing up on myself, and at least appreciating, if not celebrating, what I have done, how I am doing. I am writing this to read to you, my Parkinson's friends, because you understand my malaise and inability to move sometimes, when the chemical soup in our brains is lacking salt and garlic, when we wonder how long can this condition last. But that's the wrong question, perhaps. Maybe I need to figure out what I can do while it lasts that will make a difference in some good way. I am more than my stuck thoughts, more than a collection of regrets, grief, embarrassments, failures, and more than a seeming lack of prospects. The past and future are thoughts. The breath we take right now is the only breath we can be sure of. Being awake to the breath we are taking or letting go of is a good practice. And not too scary, after all.

Breathwork

the active
creative motion
undergoes change
in substance
weight
tending back toward
the passive
ethereal
light
wind
and belief
self and shadow
intercourse
one another
creating active balance
harmonized returning
motion
the wind
imprints
the landscape
undulations in grass
leaves
clouds
spirit dances
on in-breath
let the work
consume you

Gleaning

Close-listening
you can hear apples growing
in the orchard, skin and flesh
squeaking and stretching.

Potatoes grumble
beneath their sandy hills,
the corn silently shrugs
as the beans vine up
the grassy stalks,
bent-over ears hiding
their silken veils.

All seems
complaint of unfulfilled
intentions,
over-mature and decaying,
or too tightly held
in the knot of
ungerminated seed.

Another day, it might be
the heavy air smelling
of unspent flowers
and the muffled song
of what life is trying
to become.

Night Airs

At night I listen to the cries
of the loons and owls who come after dark
to the great pond at the edge
of the pasture.

The questions I bring are always the same:
Why am I here? Why alive?

The snail, shifting slightly
in its whorled shell at the pond's edge,
answers

    wait, wait a while

In the distance, up the bony
ridge beyond our property line,
with rough talk and feral complaints,
coyotes reply

    become as still
    as possible
    wait just a while longer

I breathe in the night air, vaporous
and heavy with the smell of wet tall grass.
Wanting more. Wanting truth.

My nostrils sting from the skunk cabbage
growing along the pond's
marshy shore, pushing the yellow
flower's thick fleshy stamen upward

continues

towards its starry conjugates
in the moonless sky.
The bulrushes whisper

    compassion needs us
    beauty needs us
    love needs us
    stay a while

I am the flower, the lily, the vast
sensate world. The ground under my feet,
substrate of silt and stone,
boulder-laden till from the last retreating glaciers,
makes a hard infertile soil.
But this is where I live, where I grow,
ready to leave my skin, to molt
completely from my thin covering
and come naked into the world again.

    love needs us
    not the other way around

the stars remind me

    wait

they implore

    wait just a little longer
    before you are gone.

before solstice

winter shadows / winter light
combine to re-invent the air

I breathe

all night the
tide pools suckle
at the moon's breast
rising and falling
in ancient rhythm

glimmer of gray
Salish Sea turns
bioluminescent
before clouds
disappear the moon

pouring water as grace

we have this whole winter
to be engulfed in dark rains
to discover Earth's
still point
in the long dream
of December

The Lushootseed Word for Salmon

At twilight,
eagle talons hook a bony
snag across the river's reach.
In the shallows,
too played out to notice or care,
swimming slowly,
not thinking ahead,
I inch my way upstream
in this salmon skin,
heavy with life and death,
crooked for a moment
against the current.
I pause in a small eddy
hidden by the shadow of a
     stone.
The ones who long ago
fished with nets along this river
know how the story goes:

Eagle's wings unfurl,
punch air downward,
his body a rising motion.
Locked in Eagle's sight,
I begin to sing the song of my
birth in this same river, times
     past.
Eagle—my brother, my father,
my teacher—dives straight
at my heart,
enters into me, into the
     dream-life,
scavenging nourishment.
Soars high above,
travels far, spreading my seed
across the green world.

Whatever Heaven

for Teresa Black (1964-2014)

What is not lost
has nothing to gain
from death. Your future,
though more or less certain,
was no better blessed
than the soul of another.

Down the road
you didn't choose
to follow just yet
lies the one holy source
we can't ever lose,
nor should ever forget.

The surprise is our love,
not the mystery of
dying itself
for we who carry loss
commending you unto
whatever heaven you love best.

We live not in
remembrance but in debt.
What is not lost
cannot be found again,
until we learn the song
of the last outgoing breath.

Ode to Geese

O dull-headed gander, goose, and gosling:
your honking—melodious as the
digital salsa ringtone
from the cell phone of a man sitting next to you
on an overbooked flight to Sacramento—
when will you fly home?

Every bleeding heart and crimson azalea
in the woodland surrounding you
lifts its blossoms skyward, in radiant silence.
Can't the three of you, or the three thousand of you,
bleat at least the same note,
up or down an octave, or harmonizing in fifths,
when you pass over my house?

It has something to do with the way you muck about
for your escargot and scum-bearded pond weeds,
nothing like the kingfisher's patient
laser-beam attack from the dead branch of a snag
onto a wild trout's boney spine in clear water.

But, okay, you are not kingfishers.
Still, there are things I like about you.
I like the flying V-formation: very cool,
very more-than or less-than,
maybe a herald of some distant victory,
or the inverted direction to heaven.

Also, I like the spontaneous takeoffs
from muddy Skagit River delta land,
where you've been eating fertile alluvial dirt
since time began.
Motionless as cabbages,
you doze until, suddenly,

Boom!

Thousands of you shift your shoulders back and up,
engaging wings, all at once and as with one mind,
with one instinctual whoosh,
your crap oozing down onto the fields, roads, and cars
instantly far beneath you, you rise
as though the earth has repelled you.

And then, wheeling high above the fields,
you vocalize your longing to be what you are not,
letting go chaotic, choking sound pulses,
the monstrous honking of a thousand coal trains,
a mournful cacophony of dissonant,
sharply inflected song, so out of touch
with this world's lavishly honed beauty
and practiced cheerfulness.

You will never be eagles.
Just geese: bullying, dumpy,
fat-assed geese. But honk for what you are,
and I will honk in return. I will put a
"Honk if you heart geese"
bumper sticker on the back of my Prius.
Brothers and sisters, honk your uniqueness
to the skies, and stand your fouled ground.

Sylvia Plath

Sylvia Plath
turned on the gas
and put her head
in the oven.
She locked her two children
inside of a room
with windows wide open
to let in the moon.
Then Sylvia Plath
turned up the gas
and following that
there was nothing.

Migration

At the corner of Lincoln
and Fraser, not far from I-5,
an old apple tree
weeps slightly northward,
away from the crowding line
of ascendant cedars
growing next to the street.
The tree is, in fact,
trying to reach
Canada.
It is taking a long time,
from spring bud
to fall's wormy harvest,
year after year.
Hundreds of apples have fallen
during the journey.
The seeds from those apples
have germinated,
becoming new ideas.
New hope.
Think about it.
One tree, an entire lifetime
moving so slowly
that I barely notice.

A Civilian Poet

for Ken, Stanley, Mallory, and Eli

I am a civilian poet,
not backed by the military
or by departments
of cultural defensiveness.

I am a conscientious objector.
While stumping for nonviolence,
I carry a gun.
I do not wear a uniform,
so you can't really tell
which side I'm on.

I am just a civilian poet
without affiliation
sniffing out the cold trail,
the odd footprint, any sign
of the brother I never knew.

I try to write away the rain
and mind the time,
keep the streets clean
for all the generations
to come.

I am a civilian poet,
searching for proof
that I existed, evidence
that I walked here on this
mountain.

I am a civilian poet,
and I know that my job could be cut
at any moment.

Part Two

Nothing and Beingness

"Nothingness lies coiled in the heart of being."

~Jean-Paul Sartre

Invocation

Don't listen for just
one voice,
nor different voices
saying the same thing.
Understand this:
each skin
has its own mouth,
each mouth has its own heart,
each heart sings its own music,
beats its own rhythm.
My voice is impatient,
burning, then cold as stones.
I have so much nothing
to say that it's hard to know
where to begin.

And when i'm gone

And when i'm gone
you'll hardly know
or may be quite perplexed
about my death
this past fortnight
and where i'm headed next

an open window to the stars
approaching at a crawl
i may be there by christmas
if i'm anywhere at all

of course i'm breathing
as i write
i can't foresee the past
for when i'm gone
i'm gone i'm gone
and i won't be the last

Who Dies?

for Stephen Levine

Remember the morning
that he walked by,
bent on teaching us
how to die?
We were on the floor
in our finest asanas,
supplicants counting breaths:
Vipassana!
"Ah, the bliss of pain," cried he,
observing the body
I thought was me.
"The bliss of comfort,"
I replied, stretching my legs
to the other side.
"That's more Buddhistic,"
he said and smiled,
shaking off death
for a little while.

"Biscuit," original watercolor by Steve Robey,
reproduced with permission of the artist.

Goat-boy

I awoke that morning to the gentle rocking of the old trailer we had hauled up from California and transplanted in a magical pasture that, amazingly, we could call ours. Dew-covered tall grass shushed as cattle browsed through nuzzling the trailer's side in the morning sun. The creek made soft noises, a sound like babies nursing. From farther away came the tinkling of bells collared on goats in the upper meadow. I took my flute and climbed from the trailer cabin, closed the door and stood smelling the sweet grassy air, taking in the lightest beginnings of a breeze. I walked to the creek and followed it away from the trailer, looked back once to watch a cow rubbing old muscles and bone against the door. Then I turned to walk up the hill, laughing, to serenade the goats, thin creatures with yellow eyes, their song harsh, their scent dank and feral, who awaited my arrival.

Dream

I am sitting on a bench in Stanley Park
with Eckhart Tolle. He chuckles to himself
at the irony of existence. I know what he means.
No one can grasp the world, which you'd think
a four-year-old could do, because there is
no world to grasp. Eckhart finds this
amusing.

We can know our bedrooms, our garden,
a book, an illness, our kids somewhat.
Beyond that, it's anybody's guess.
Always trying to grasp, we wake
empty-handed. People are lovely, but
humanity is insanity.
As Descartes meant to say,
"I think. Therefore I drink."

dreams

If I knew what dreams were
I'd be in one
at this very moment.
Do you say of someone,
"She had a way with dreams?"

Life

I look for it every day,
ask other people
about it.

"Have you seen Life?"
I ask a woman in a gray coat.

As she edges past me
I realize this may not be
the best way
to go about looking for life.

Seeking truth

Even with my clever brain
and two opposing thumbs,
I couldn't say without a doubt
where what we call the truth is from.
While talking to a friend today,
I looked around and knew again
that truth is not that easily found.
It may not even be around.

Beside my bed

Beside my bed
the doctor said,
"So you really want
to die?"
He didn't have a verb
for nonexistence,
but keeps me
here alive
at his insistence.
It's not like God said,
"Go extend
your lifespan."
The doctor told me,
"If God won't do it,
I can."

Move over, Mother

for Karen Cook

Move over, Mother.
Make me room
inside the vastness
of God's body,
in the quiet gospel
of your womb.
Religion doesn't know
my destination.
Frustration, boredom,
grief, rejection
occur at any intersection.
While all the colors
of the coat I wear
to lay me down
help me find my place
somewhere
upon the frozen ground.

Someone left open

Someone left open
the gate, and now
there is chaos:
chairs crashing into tables,
snakes mingling
with cats,
good ideas getting confused
with bad ideas.
Whoever opened the gate,
did they know this
might happen?

No one knows

No one knows
we're here.
No one is really sure
who we are.
We can't avoid Them—
on the sidewalk,
for example.
None among us
pledges allegiance
to the concept of the One
because the Whole
is an illusion
and, too, no one
is really here,
anyway.

I looked into the woods

I looked into the woods today,
a sunlit path I travel down,
exploring every cranny's part,
miles of darkness in my heart.
And when I looked inside my soul,
I found it wanting,
on the whole.

I saved a mouse

I saved a mouse
from the pool today.
He shook it off
and ran away,
up to the woods
where the animals sat,
the owl and the 'coon
and the big gray cat.
I cried and cried
till I felt cried out
when the mouse decided
to take that route.

Staring out the window

Staring out the window,
suddenly I realize
there is nothing to write.
When you look at yourself
in the mirror for a long time,
do you notice how you become
some other creature
entirely?

Nice people should not write

Nice people should not write.
They've better things to do.
I've often said
"I write sometimes.
I only need a good first line."

Instead of writing,
I suggest you learn to cook,
but only if you do not write a book
about GMOs and gluten
or the diet of Vladimir Putin.

Make music. Celebrate your life.
Try oil painting with your wife.
But please don't be absurd!
Don't write a single word.

Keep pen and paper out of sight.
Nice people should not write.
Especially late at night.

I live in a

I live in a
nice green
garbage bin,
in the morning
it's toast and tea.
Where I live there
aren't any
goblins or dreams,
just the garbage,
the rats,
and me.

death 1.

What lies beyond the fence?
It's everybody's question,
but no one knows the first thing
about how to land on the other side,
in rank grass strewn with rusted pieces
of barbed wire and broken glass.
It's one possibility.

death 2.

Who was Jesus?
How the hell would I know?
I know only about what's inside my head
and I don't even know
where that comes from.
Do I believe in Jesus?
What's to believe?
At the moment of my death
I will sing out either
"Sweet Jesus" or "My God"
or maybe "Oh, boy!"

death 3.

I feel liberated by the idea of death.
Is it my death that everyone is being
so nice about? Is that
what death is like?

Out in the garden

Out in the garden
at the end of the world
all by herself sits a nice little girl.
Maybe she'll meet a nice little friend,
who is always alone and always outside,
and is perfectly happy to stay till the end.
Together they make such a nice little pair,
the girl and her friend sitting each in a chair.

Fathers and Sons

The father and the son look out
at one another across a great distance.
They are miles apart.
Miles miles miles.
No light shines down upon them.
They are perhaps a million miles apart.
More than that. They are in separate
galaxies.

The son said something
about a thousand years ago that is
halfway across space to the waiting father.
The father is about to raise his hand
but decides to wait for another
millennium. He is very tired.
He will move his hand in a few centuries,
he decides.

The father will eat breakfast
after a period of time comparable
to the span between the Pleistocene
and the twentieth century has passed.
He hears rumbling in his stomach,
as though glaciers were moving slowly
across a continent. He thinks
he hears something in the distance,
from some other galaxy?

His ears move like folds of strata
pushing upward, but he is not sure,
not certain where his son has gone.

Breaking Up

I am trying to reach you via Skype
but there are issues. Sounds and images
from my end break loose skyward,
bang against satellites and asteroids,
slam-bam back to me, dear, not to you.

No big surprises there.
You Tweeted some sweet cold sleet
hitting me in the face, burning cold.
I thought our talking points were moot;
was there not a misconception
misdirected to this corner of creation,
clogged with vast pools of dark matter?

Somehow I've lost the backbeat,
the thrumming of my blood
trying to reconcile our structural
instability, find the geodesic
architecture that will help us cohere.

Tried to reach you through the grapevine
instead of on the land line.
But the signal's breaking up.
I think I'm losing you.

Last Words?

My final thought
might be:
I will have more to say
now that I am no longer
using words.

Part Three

Telling the Story

"Have you thought of a story? I was asked each morning, and each morning I was forced to reply with a mortifying negative."

~*Mary Shelley*
Introduction to 1831 edition of *Frankenstein*

Berkeley Pit,
Butte, Montana, in 1974

Big sky white,
low ceilinged,
hung over with emptiness,
the pit mine
deep as hell,
and me standing
on the lip.

Town dogs snarl
as I pass dark winter houses,
still nowhere to go,
still unbelieving
the truth of it.
Not the town,
but the unbridled
space
that lacks
reasonable shape
or meaning. Emptiness
on this scale bodes ill.

No one
can tell me
its raw history,
the why of it,
the unburied truth
lying at the bottom of
seeping bad water,
or how what once
filled the hole
before there was a hole
benefitted anyone
in particular.

The author across the border, on the Okanogan River,
British Columbia, Canada (1977).

Crossing the Border

Morning

From the country west of Edmonton,
last light,
the smells of bread and campfire smoke
inside the car all night.
Sleeping over at Wild Horse Lake,
having seen bear, coyote
and heard birds calling across the water;
three Albertan fishermen had given us their report,
one trout that gleamed from the fire
as they walked past our camp,
hanging at one man's side like a knife
before they climbed into the pickup
and disappeared back towards the Jasper highway.
We ate soup and rice,
finishing together as the wind rose, and then
burrowing all night out of it inside the sleeping bags,
making love as the wind shushes our moans,
then my head just above the food box:
honey, bread, and our salts and spices for
cooking in the alder-wood fires;
smoke in my clothes and hair,
the scent my bone grey sweater
has absorbed after nights of bending down
to blow on coals and make the flames
lick up into the bottom of the
blue metal pots holding soup

continues

that ashes drift into
like quiet thoughts from the lake we rise to watch,
now that it's morning.

Gathering

just dry sticks for the fire, north of Peyto Lake,
then Yoho; along a river
branches snap and the bear looks up.
Water walks behind me,
over stones and old campsites.
The bear's claws pry at the darkened window,
my mouth goes dry as the stale bread he smells,
the bread that I made in Seattle, and ate,
that he wants to devour, and I want
to trade him for the thin blue cloth
of the tent we lie beneath / that I breathe under,
hearing his claws at the windshield
seeing an eye reflected in the rear view mirror
that I look through / seeing morning / where he
crushes a branch of the rose-hips
and tugs loose the handle on the camp water pump
and crosses the river, grumbling
his hump back among his rocks and trees.
You do not need any protecting.
I never really understood you.

Washington

South and west across the border,
still north of Omak,
in dry-mouth country. In the shimmering heat
of America, I see you taking a different road.
None of this is spoken.
Driving past old homesteads still standing,
ribs of weather-darkened Ponderosa pines
growing in hot-rock canyons, we wonder
if the bald front tire will get us back to Seattle.
The road is straighter here after the mountains,
the wood drier for burning in fires along the coast.
The ranches still going
holed in dry scrub hollows well back from any road.
A distant line of cottonwoods
marks the path of the Okanogan River that flows by the town
where Little Ron was born and called
the white lady Grandmother.

Dear Jesus

On Jamie Little Boy's fourth birthday, the twenty-third of August, 1967, he is in Omak, Washington. The day is important because he learns that day that he will have a new home. Mama White Hair says so, and Grandma, as Jamie also calls her, has never lied to him. He wonders if there will be a party with lots of people making happy sounds and singing Happy Birthday to him while he sits on a kind of throne, just a little higher up than anyone else in the room.

Little Boy is so excited, in fact, that he pees in his pants right in front of Mama White Hair, which sometimes happens to him. He hopes he will not pee his pants when he meets his new family.

Little Boy and Grandma take a Greyhound bus to Spokane, where they drink root beer from a soda machine inside the bus depot.

"Is this it, Grandma?"

"No," Mama White Hair says, "this is not the place."

Outside the bus station, the withering heat sears the trees along the sidewalk. They have to get on another bus to reach the Social Services office.

Little Boy will remember this day when he is a grown man attending his first AA meeting in Seattle. On his fourth birthday, he doesn't really even know that he is an Indian. There is no party, no cake, and he wonders where he is going.

They wait patiently at the reception desk for a few minutes and are then shown into a featureless room with a small table and some chairs. There is a kind-looking woman who stands up to greet Jamie Little Boy. After she says hello, Little Boy looks up at Mama White Hair for guidance. Grandma's eyes have fixed on a photograph of the president, Lyndon B. Johnson. That and a calendar still on the June page are the only objects attached to the wall. The calendar picture shows a clear-running river rushing past forests of fir and cedar under a blue sky.

The next few moments are confusing for Little Boy. A man and a woman enter the room. He glances at their faces and looks at the floor, concentrating to not pee. Not now. The man and woman try to engage Little Boy in conversation, but he either looks up at Mama White Hair or down on the floor.

A few phrases register: *your new parents, this is going to work, good for a first visit.*

This marks the beginning of the first life that Jamie Little Boy can remember.

Rain

On the sidewalk outside the food coop, gray red-footed
pigeons dip their beaks, picking up crumbs from
gluten-free muffins with the speed and efficiency of
a good typist. Discarded cellophane wrappers
scratch along the sidewalk in the dry wind.
The pigeons stride to their next morsel, heads bobbing
back and forth on short necks, expressions dim, poker-

faced. They remind me of the barnyard hens I tended
for Grandpa, Mom's dad, back in Minnesota. After we
moved west, near Seattle, Grandpa held on a few more
indifferent years, but my mom was reborn, re-spirited.
I remember how she used to feed wildlife outside
our home: raccoons, deer, feral cats, pintail ducks,
great blue herons, even eagles. A decade before her
death, she began to pray for rain during

long dry spells. "The animals suffer," she would say.
Like St. Francis, she often carried a small bird
in her open palm. She prayed, waited, and rejoiced
when the deluge began. I miss her strength, her
loving ministrations to the earth, her belief
that was deeper than superstition. I miss her in this
moment as I hear distant waters gathering, see pigeons
eating crumbs on another warm, cloudless day.

Escaping the Glass

Behind the dormer window
a white shroud flutters.
The windows are locked.
No one could enter.
She lies waiting
beneath the green rooftop
moving her eyes and lips.
This morning
the wind presses
against the window,
and the scratching of muslin
on the glass,
wanting out,
answers.

If only

He somewhat favors twilight
when lavender and sage
scent the laden air with perfume
from a garden, there, just up the street.
Not in any hurry, in rhythm
with a summer eve,
easy as old cats,

he slowly shuffles past the house where
the mother and five children live,
turns slowly in his mind to see
the tired kiss she gives to each,
putting them to bed,
rocking them to sleep.

The garden he once knew
is gone, left untended by his hand,
but children live
and gather strength,
not for working plots of earth,
or seeing us as trusted guides.
They're looking for tall trees to climb.

And when the evening calls him out,
he can't un-think the peace he'd find
atop the curving stairs
as one by one the children say the prayers
they've memorized by heart.
When behind their bedroom window
the bedside lamps go dark.

Whatever might be said
about this misbegotten day,
the fallen star, now embers,
the children home and safe,
are dreaming in their beds
about another, wilder place.

The Lehmans

They died up roads
named after themselves,
far from town, their mailboxes
knocked over like downed cattle.
Their souls still inhabit
the rusted-out Chevys in the yard,
long after the engines have stopped
and them, too.

It's like you can't even walk
up their roads anymore
because of death.

How I Got Here

The first deer wander down by
my place to eat windfall apples
in the old orchard.
I planted those apple trees,
way back when. I've lived here
a long time.

Once we tried to cut
all the red cedar down.
There were all these spirits
at my back; they hid in the woods
or out in the water.
Orca, coyote, raven.
Even the stones had spirits:
some good, some bad.
Just like people.

Some of those old trees survived,
and they became my ancestors.
Back then, oysters clogged
the shoreline. Their shells became
this white-sand beach.

We told lots of jokes
about things that could harm us,
like the jealous husband who died
and came back as a mosquito.
After that, we laughed
whenever we slapped mosquitos.

continues

I dreamed I was flying over
the water, could see the great Tahoma,
way off. Hit the water, went under,
and became a salmon.
I could see clear
to where I was born,
up a shallow creek off
the Nooksack. That's the spot
where I'll die.

When people came,
the Madrone trees arched
high above their greasy camps.
After that things were really different.

The voices that tell people
to do good in the world
are hidden deep in thick tree-bark.
The deer are struggling
from their graves,
for this is a time of little food.

Just before I leave here,
Heron flies by, says,
"You should not…"

That's all I could hear
before the wind grabbed Heron's voice,
put it in a cedar box,
and blew west.

* * *

I sit against the trunk of an old cedar, looking out at the distant smoke rising from the fire somewhere to the south. Below me, on the rocks near the salt water, Man-Who-Takes-Trees is doing something strange: drinking salt water, then gagging and spitting it back up. He keeps doing that until I finally can't stand it any more.

"Takes Trees!" I call. "Why are you trying to drink salt water?" He looks up at me, eyes gleaming, yells back, "Look, the tide

continues

is really way out there. I want to be ready if it doesn't come back in. I am practicing salmon breathing!"

Takes-Trees goes back to his drinking and vomiting.

Children are frightened of his strange, mossy appearance. They walk quickly, keep looking over their shoulders to see whether Man-Who-Takes-Trees is quietly following them and might pick one of them out for roasting over a cedar fire. They find the stones he has piled, one on top of another.

When Man-Who-Takes-Trees drinks salt water, because the tide may never flow again, because all the streams may run dry, I think he is no fool. Once he told me that if this place goes dry, all of creation is done for.

* * *

The island across the water has no name, but I name the clouds, each cloud a different name. Seabirds in large groups soar and squawk, feeding in the rich chaos of the sea currents. I call that Life.

When I was growing up, school made me feel like I was like drowning. I daydreamed, named clouds, like the one who looked like my uncle, twisted and humped with palsy. I named that cloud Water-Goes-Slow.

Started drinking hard liquor in junior high. Years later I came back to this place, to come into my power. Then all that bad stuff stopped. But it took the efforts of many people: my family, the police, a mental-health counselor, my elders. Not too much my peers, who were teen-agers too. Ones-who-died.

Now, when the sky turns gray, like the smooth weathered tree trunks tossed to the top of the tide line, I become like a mountain, strong in my heart. I've been trying to find a story in the driftwood, a vision.

I remember a time in my youth when my brothers paddled towards shore. I stood on the oyster-shell beach. In the shallows, the water was turquoise. I heard drums all around me, talking to spirits: All this had been created: rocks, fish, water, clouds, red cedar, what we need to live. All this was here.

I know where the sun is going to rise. How can people know that, and still lose their way?

Me & Woody Guthrie

I said to the man in the mirror,
"Woody Guthrie was my father."
My real dad was as cold as the metal rung
of the ladder I grabbed
as Woody and I rode free on the Santa Fe Dustbowl Special
westbound out of Alamogordo, New Mexico.

I reveled in the sweet desert smell, the abalone-shell dawn,
my skin frozen onto the steel, the freshness and danger of life.
Limitless opportunity for everybody in this good land
rising anew out of loss and despair.

Woody carried his guitar in its baggy case slung over his shoulder.
Just last night he taped a sticker on the front of his guitar
that says "This machine kills fascists."
That got some looks.

Hanging on until we hit the border and the train slowed,
Woody nervous about the yard bulls and wanting to lickety-split.
I hovered above the rails, my feet numb, and I finally cried
about my mother's death back in the last century.

Once, after she died, I discovered a box
containing handwritten letters from my mother to Jesus.
They all began "Dear Jesus," or "Dear Lord."
They were like prayers I felt too embarrassed to read.
I thought I should feel some specific emotion.

I cried for my mother before jumping with stiff legs
onto the railroad siding, following Woody,
then veering off, limping in a different direction
towards the new day.

Farm Bulletin for Vancouver, B.C.

nothing doing, he cried
just like that the old boy grabbed a ride
in the night and rain
couldn't talk
had to coarse-whisper
'cause his voice was gone
headed away from here
came from ground, rain, night
riderless dark
began falling away from the tail lights
came headed the other way
crippled like this, see
and near mute too
so his thumb hooked down
and his feet
they scraped that gravel & didn't move
until I said, hardly able to talk myself,
there you go, chum
giving him everything

Billy the Kid's Last Ride

The kid, his head kiltered to one side,
sat the wheelchair like it was a king's throne.
He said to me,

When does the next bus come by here?

We were on a river somewhere,
in Wyoming maybe,
and it was Jew-lie the fourth,
some years past.

That youngster is a Calamity

purred the coffee-gossip ladies
from town.
True, he was upon some hard times.
Kept saying,

When does the next bus come by here?
I been waiting and waiting.

Calamity Jane his mom.
Legs like two gun barrels
that could shoot sparks,
if the mood suited.
I said to him,
"I've seen you running to catch my bus."

The kid's head leaned harder,
near-parallel with the rust-red dirt
below our feet.

But what time's the bus come by today?

he repeated.
We were on the edge of a canyon.
I focused on small nearby things
such as the spider
on the scrub juniper tree.
He sat his wheelchair like it was
a Warm-blood mare,
tipped his broad-brimmed hat.

You don't think those ladies'll shoot me, do you?

My legs began to stiffen,
in condolence, I suppose.
My arms, then my fingers,
chest, heart.
I tilted my head to one side,
sat down in my wheelchair.
It was like getting situated
on a buggy seat
in the 1870s. Somewhere in
Wyoming maybe.

Once more, his reedy voice
asking,

When does the next bus come by here?
I been waiting and waiting.

Halfway Point

The Tetons disappeared
in early October,
devoured by high-voltage
charcoal clouds
tearing apart the Gallatins
and Yellowstone.

On the western slope,
east of Driggs,
my son guided me up a rocky,
snow-skiffed trail that
puddled and froze,
took off upland from Teton Creek
towards the pass south
of the Wigwams.

My fingers started biting from the
wet cold through my too-thin
gloves.

"I can see how people could
die out here," I said.

My son, at thirty
a little less than half my age,
took it as a question.
"People don't know when to
turn around, admit that today
isn't the day."

I used to think I knew what I was doing
in the woods, on mountainsides.
Maybe I did. I am still alive.
I have stories, some worth saving,
others I would rather forget.

The wind changed direction
and we both noticed the sudden
temperature drop. Looking at the sky,
at each other, we turned,
the cold wind now in our faces.

Snow came harder as we
wordlessly started the long hike
back to the truck.

Why I Am Not a Cowboy

Once I was more water than bone.
Young and thirsty with vague ambition.
I left home early, headed west.
Got jobs—dug fencepost holes outside
Elko, Nevada; cut buffalo calves
out of the herd on horseback in
the Yellowstone; excavated shallow graves
in the hard-pan soil of the Blue Mountains,
up on the Oregon Trail.

Skipped straight ahead into the middle of life,
a smooth, flat stone on calm water.

I've got two grown kids and an ex-wife.
Edna and I met, then married,
out on the edge of Boise. It proved,
for a time, sweet succor for a blue cowboy.
That's when I started to drink
and it's why I stopped, too.
Sober for sixteen years now.
Edna called it too little too late,
but I know it saved my life.

Despite an edgy restlessness
and a desire for cold beer, I have retained
an arid sense of optimism.
When it rains around here, well,
to me it's mostly a dry rain.

I wear the discarded clothing of certain
dead cowboys; snap-button plaid shirts,
leather chaps, spurs the size
of a mountain lion's paw—
the sartorial essence
of America's cowboy dream.
It's a way to whistle in the dark
past the graveyard in my home town.
Don't think I'm not scared
of dying there.

I miss home, kids, family.
Now and then, the sharp-toed leather boots
that once belonged to some old boy
end up riding my feet.
The life requires a desperation that I
tip my hat to as I ride on past.
I still wonder if I could have done it
different, maybe better, given half a chance.

Fences

I've built fences that
I never crossed.
It takes a long time to go
around them,
because they stretch
for miles. I found
old bone-dry wood
for the posts and poles,
banging everything
together with
antebellum spikes and nails.
My fences go in all directions,
nothing too organized.
I built every one myself.

Some Facts of Life

This is just me, what I've done:

I've hitched rides from drunks, climbed the dark tower, invited doorbell evangelists in for a beer, been struck dumb by beauty, rode a bike, got hit by a car, travelled with men and women just out of prison. Got ripped, threw up, believed Ayn Rand, and quit college basketball.

Since you're interested, I'm just giving you some plain facts, as well as I can remember them.

No time was harder for me than being a kid. That's when huge things get lost forever, good pieces of who you are, or it's where new lies are glued into your brain. It's your fault, I didn't want you, I'm ashamed of you, but *I worry all the time about you.*

I flew to Iceland to escape being worried over and sat on a fishing dock in the sun. I fled from human kindness and hospitality, couldn't find the girl in the *National Geographic* photo swinging a pitchfork full of hay into a wagon, her hair blonde, her cheeks red, the sun favoring every feature. She's the reason I went.

I drank whiskey at a picnic table in the misting fog of Seattle's waterfront, looked out the window of my room next to the Alaskan Way viaduct, and watched who went past at two in the morning. Had coffee with whores at midnight, slept with my brother-in-law's daughter there once, played guitar and sang Woody Guthrie songs for money on Pike Street, disappointed my parents, and painted giant vegetables on the wall.

My friend's father Doc took us to breakfast from time to time. We went to weird all-night places and ate ravenously. Thick brown-sugared baked beans, leather-belt-thick slices of bacon, white bread

continues

toast with butter and jam, steaming short stacks of buttermilk cakes, tumblers of orange juice, and enough coffee to float us until the following Tuesday.

Doc was good, a country physician who read literature. Maybe he understood what me and his son Country were trying to do, but I don't think so. We didn't have a clear vision ourselves, just shot the movie and put the film in the can, sealing it with wax. Never even developed the negative. It's still out there somewhere, maybe nailed to a wall.

Doc and his wife Ginger had two sons, Country and Joel, and two beautiful daughters, Joan and Kipper. The kids grew up on an island, but later Joan lived in my apartment building, upstairs, and her hair smelled like apricot shampoo. She's the one who told me about my brother's plane crash near Issaquah. I didn't have a phone.

My grandfather, Mom's dad, worked at the grain elevator in Red Wing. My dad managed a hardware store in Spokane. His dad was a streetcar conductor in Minneapolis, an immigrant from Germany.

There was a time I spent staring at the ceiling, totally lost. I wrote a screenplay, got a bit part as a walk-on in a movie made from a Joan Didion novel, and dated an actress whose crooked smile occupied her face the same way that her body inhabited the camera frame in her movies. Country, meanwhile, wrote a review of *Deep Throat*, which was playing in a porn house on Pike Street. Like it was a normal movie. The *Seattle Times* ran his review. That was the year my brother jumped off the Space Needle with a parachute, just two years before the plane crashed.

I was kept back a grade in elementary school. I sill have cognitive deficits.

Years passed. Horses burned in a barn fire and wild pigs gave birth on steep hillsides. Nothing worked out romantically for a while, unless you consider repeatedly getting sucked in and spit out by love "working out." Country went to work in Hollywood and lived in Poway just north of San Diego. When I told him on the phone that I had Parkinson's he sounded shocked, which surprised me. We haven't spoken since. There is Parkinson's in Hollywood, for example, Michael J. Fox, Robin Williams, Katherine Hepburn. It's not like it doesn't happen.

Country and I had played together on the high school basketball team. I got an offer from a college following a good senior season and left the next year. Later, when we met up again in Seattle in our twenties, Country gave me sage advice one morning in our apartment kitchen, where I sat drinking coffee, complaining about my job. He said, "Maybe you could get a better job if you finished your degree." I did that, and to this day thank him for the push. But I didn't know he'd one day abandon me as a friend. My best friend.

Mexico. I went there. Too bright, way too much color to take in through the eyes. Duluth, where Grandpa worked before he and Grandma moved to Red Wing, was more to my liking. Fifty-seven degrees and raining in mid-July. Coming from Atlanta, my wife and me and our infant son all happy in our 1978 VW camper, we hit Highway 2 in the cooling weather in the land of ten thousand lakes and turned left.

I've lost track of lost loves, been a monk and a spiritual supplicant, worked for a living, made a fool of myself, and read condensed novels I bought at garage sales in Calgary. I've never nearly died and wonder what it is with the tunnel of light. I've never been back to Iceland but have floated in the waters of the Great Salt Lake, absolving me of my sins while I learned to float by faith alone.

Part Four

The Pluto Chronicles

"So how long does it take to get to Pluto? Roughly 9–12 years."

~ *Fraser Cain,* astronomy guy

Club Pluto

"Let's go to Pluto," I said casually to my wife the other day. "We need to really get away, and if we left next Monday we would be there in about nine years."

It was the day after images of the dwarf planet had been received from NASA's New Horizons spacecraft. I expected my wife to wrinkle her nose at my suggestion and send me off to take a shower and put on my NASA clean-room suit, but instead she looked at me with interest.

"Seriously?" she asked.

"Yes, seriously," I said. "It has an atmosphere and useful elements like nitrogen and ice, and also a very low rate of skin cancer."

"I'll bet it's colder than a relief pitcher's butt in the bullpen," she mumbled.

"You'd rather burn up here on Earth?" I asked.

"I'm just saying…"

I tried to find a crack in her resistance. "We don't need much fuel to get there. We can use large planets along the way as gravity slingshots, and also we could limit our power consumption by not listening to too many audiobooks."

My wife looked surprised. "Well, aren't we Stephen Hawking today. Gravity slingshots, no less."

I blushed. "I've been thinking about this all night. I'm not saying it would be easy."

"Well, what would we do with Elfo and Springtime? Somebody's got to take care of them while we're gone. Springtime's litter-box?" she said with a challenging question mark.

continues

I was flummoxed. Could a ten-year-old doofus golden Lab and a pathetically needy gray tabby cat possibly keep us from moving to another planet if we wanted to?

"Let's give the pets to our children," I suggested.

Our kids, thank goodness, are grown and live in Montana and South Carolina. They would barely notice our absence, except for the nonreturnable animals.

"Look, honey. The science is good. I trust NASA; I trust NOVA and the whole PBS thing; I trust those astronomers at Johns Hopkins; and I trust Viking River Cruises, a major public television contributor."

"What if we miss?" my wife asked.

"Miss the famous dwarf planet? Then I guess it's Hello Kuiper Belt," I said cheerfully. "Seriously, dear, I think we can get there. We've at least got a snowball's chance on an asteroid."

Digitalia

I remember the heady early days of the Internet, when it was exciting to enter the welcoming site of a new online library catalog or stumble accidentally into a classified U.S. military munitions depot database. Getting a username and password was like a teen-ager being handed the keys to a nuclear submarine. "Don't stay out too late, honey," my mom might say. "And for crying out loud don't start any new wars!"

Those days are gone. In fact, I'm downright uncomfortable with the direction that the Digital Revolution is taking us. Will it be over soon?

In the Age of Information, it looks like we're talking to ourselves much of the time. We spend hours walking city streets and haunting the aisles of grocery stores, our eyes on the digital devices we hold, music pouring through earbuds into our brains. The current advanced stage of the social media epidemic has even drawn the attention of the *AARP Magazine*, which recently published an article on the five dangers of chronic smart-phone use. I'll spare you the details.

What has digital technology actually done for us, or to us? Indeed, use of online social media, in particular, has been linked to rising suicide rates, vaping, and Donald Trump's presidential campaign.

I'll admit that I can't Tweet my way out of a paper bag, don't use Facebook or Instagram or Tumblr, nor do I get Linked-in, do deviantART, Tag, or even bother to clean out some of the 412,985 e-mails languishing in my in-box.

continues

I'm not proud of my record. I come from a long line of technology-challenged people; my roots go back to German mystics in the Rheinland. A self-described Boring Person and Luddite, my few friends are all like, "No! No! You're a really interesting speller!" The simple truth about me is that I'm out-technologied by a pair of pliers, my typing skills are shot, and the term "social medium" brings to mind a fortune-teller who plays Mahjong at the senior center.

But there's more than cognitive ability and thumb-driven keyboarding aptitude involved here. We may be connected as all get out—and maybe I'm just rationalizing my own misgivings about the whole 24/7-connection thing—but is anybody asking why we need to be so intimately conjoined at the USB port, or if it's a good thing?

I know I'm in the impact zone of the revolution, so it's small wonder that I feel that I have to apologize and berate myself as though I were a pathetic clown unable to use any device more complicated than a fork, while my friend Kristin sounds almost guilty because she's having such fun with her digital gadgets and is so good at using them.

We decided to buy a computer late in the last century after we discovered our eight-year-old son trying to find the Internet by spinning the washer and dryer knobs out in the utility room. We decided to buy a Macintosh. The first one, a Mac Quadra 605, had 4 Mb of RAM.

I had been under the impression that Macs were supposed to be so easy to use, but words like "plug-'n-play," "out of the box," "online in seconds" (to chat gaily!) were not written to enlighten people from my generation. I upped my dose of Clonazepam when we brought home Mac the First, treating the unpacking process reverently, as though there were a collection of first-edition Harry Potter books inside. My cluelessness about the journey upon which we were embarking made me realize I had missed an important class: "How Not To Act Like A Technology Stupidhead."

My wife got me to talk to my neurologist about my, what, learning disability? My neurologist is a short woman of South Korean descent who interned in Memphis, Tennessee, and professes to have a keen taste for hominy grits. Her name, unbelievably, is Dr. Small. Dr. Small turned me over to Dr. Psychologist to run me through some cognitive tests. That was unsettling; surely they'd discover I had Alzheimer's disease. I could only think: Will my wife remember to buy beer before the Super Bowl when I've forgotten how to work the TV remote?

The high point of the interview was when the psychologist asked me to spell "world" backwards. This seemed somehow critical to my evaluation. If you can spell "world" backwards, apparently you're qualified to become the CEO of a major corporation, or at least president of the United States. To underscore the importance of this key capability, public schools must adopt a policy requiring children and teens to study hard to prepare for standardized tests leading to careers in companies that need people, good people, who can spell backwards.

I passed the "world" test.

Since I obviously have nothing better to do, I recently set up an experiment to test the efficacy of one tiny piece of digitalia: a smart text editor. I typed, or at least thought I had, the following text at moderate speed and without making any corrections. "I'd rather have a full bottle in front of me than a full frontal lobotomy."

continues

Can't argue with that. Due to my keyboarding ineptness, though, I'd actually written, "I'd rather hasbe a full bottle I feront of methen y fullferomtal lobotopmu."

That's correct, I can boast the same touch-typing accuracy level as Lowly Worm.

To fix the mistakes, I ran the uncorrected version through my computer's automatic spelling and grammar repair shop, thus creating the statement, "I'd rather hassle a full bottle in ferret of me than a full femoral lavatory."

Actually, I was relieved that the results of my neurological exam showed only borderline cognitive impairment in a couple areas of brain function. So why beat myself up about being a dummy when it comes to things of a high-tech nature? I'm obviously damaged goods. I'll leave the Information Age to the Digital Revolutionaries who love it so much.

Meanwhile, I think I'll go out into the utility room to see if I can contact a lost civilization on Pluto using the dials on the clothes dryer. Oh, I just remembered, we upgraded to a digital washer-dryer when our son left home the first year of the new millennium. I tried but failed to understand the new digital washtub. There were no dials. Drat!

"There is a feeling of happiness that I do not deserve."

Uncle Walt

I wrote a fictional story, which was to be included herein, about the dotage of a famous cartoon rodent whose name I will not write down on paper. Why won't I write the name? Because I'm paranoid.

Okay, Uncle Walt, I concede. *Nolo contendere*. I am not going to put that story into the book. My editor has convinced me that once *my* book is available from Amazon, I would be hearing from Disney copyright infringement attorneys. Bent on protecting this rodent's squeaky-clean reputation, they would not take kindly to my literary violation of Uncle Walt's intellectual property.

You probably know of whom I speak.

So I caved. "Take it out," I said.

Thus: not a word from me about rumored drinking problems, financial misjudgment, or dementia. No "insider" nuggets regarding a love for reading "Talk of the Town" in the *New Yorker*, old Alan Alda movies and Japanese kabuki theater. I will simply shut up and not mention the great desire to make an action buddy movie with Steve McQueen, and the great disappointment and sadness at Mr. McQueen's death.

I wonder sometimes about Pluto, though, the mute but amiable mutt Uncle Walt created in 1930. (I think I can write the word *Pluto* without fear of legal reprisal.)

Now here's something freaky: The *same year* Uncle Walt sketched his Pluto into life, astronomer Clyde Tombaugh discovered Pluto the planet, which was taken into the celestial fold as, to Earthlings, the ninth planet from the sun. At least until astronomy guys downgraded Pluto to kitty-barf status because, they averred, there were asteroids without names in the Kuiper Belt that were just as big, or bigger, than Pluto the planet, and who were, in scientific terms, a lot funnier.

Uncle Walt was probably not around when Pluto did a stint as the Roman god of the underworld, not long before Bob Dylan was born, but the fact that in 1930 both Pluto the planet was "discovered" and Pluto the cartoon dog was "created" has conspiracy written all over it. What is Uncle Walt hiding?

There. I've gotten it off my chest and I didn't break any laws. Did I?

Grand Teton National Park, many border crossings later.
(Leslie Tregillus photo)

RICK HERMANN is the author of two previous books: *The Bright World of Dandelion Court* and *Parkinson's Dreams about Me: My Dance with the Shaking Palsy.* He was born in St. Maries, Idaho, and has lived in Southern California; Atlanta, Georgia; and Seattle, Index, and Clinton, Washington. He moved to Whatcom County in 1987 with his wife Lee Willis, where they raised their son, Eli Hermann, in the city of subdued excitement.

Made in the USA
Charleston, SC
09 December 2016